FOLK SONGS OF GOA
Mando-Dulpods & Deknnis

Song of Goa, no. 3

José Pereira, Micael Martins &
António da Costa

FOLK SONGS OF GOA

Mando-Dulpods & Deknnis

ARYAN BOOKS INTERNATIONAL
NEW DELHI

FOLK SONGS OF GOA
Mando-Dulpods & Deknnis

ISBN-81-7305-280-8 (HB)
ISBN-81-7305-281-6 (PB)

First Published in **2005** by :

ARYAN BOOKS INTERNATIONAL
Pooja Apartments, 4B, Ansari Road, New Delhi - 110 002 (India)
Tel.: 23287589, 23255799, Fax: 91-11-23270385
E-mail: aryanbooks@vsnl.com

This work has been sponsored by

THE GOAN OVERSEAS ASSOCIATION OF NEW SOUTH WALES, AUSTRALIA

Computer Typeset at ABI Prints & Publishing Co., New Delhi
Printed in India at B.B.N. Printers, New Delhi

THIS BOOK IS DEDICATED
TO THE CHERISHED MEMORY
OF STUDENTS OF GOAN SONG
WHO DEVOTED THEIR LIVES
TO THE PRESERVATION OF OUR RICH HERITAGE

MOST OF ALL TO
MICAEL MARTINS (1914-1999)

BUT ALSO TO
AGAPITO MIRANDA (1911-1995)
LÚCIO RODRIGUES (1915-1973)
AND
ANTÓNIO MASCARENHAS (1916-1993)

PRAESTA QUAESUMUS
OMNIPOTENS MISERICORS DEUS
UT ANIMAE FAMULORUM TUORUM
LUCIS PERPETUAE
TE MISERANTE
RECIPIANT BEATITUDINEM

CONTENTS

TYPES AND SUBTYPES OF KONKANI SONG

I. RELIGIOUS SONGS
1. *Fugrhi* [1]
2. *God-dde Ramayann* [2]
3. *Launnim* [3]
4. Sacred art song, Christian [4]
5. Sacred art song, Hindu [5]
6. Sacred folk song, Christian [6]
7. Sacred folk song, Hindu [7]
8. *Zoti* [8]

II. CHILDHOOD SONGS
1. Child songs [9]
2. Childrens' songs [10]
3. *Duvallo* [11]
4. *Palnnam* [12]

III. MARRIAGE SONGS
1. Brahmin nuptial chants [13]
2. Kunnbi nuptial chants [14]
3. *Ovi/Vers/Zoti* [15]
4. Shudra/Sudir nuptial chants [16]
5. *Shobhane* [17]

IV. DEATH SONGS
1. *Banvarh* [18]

PREFACE

Konkani, the language of Goan Song, appears to have been in existence by the 11th century. For as long as we have a record, its speakers have been impassioned lovers of music, and if their ancestors, at the time when the Konkani language originated, were singing songs in it, then Goan Song would have been in existence for ten continuous centuries. But whatever has survived of these songs is fast disappearing, their fragile melodies drowned by the noise blaring from the electronic maws of radio and television. It is unfortunate that these songs, as surviving in the 19th and 20th centuries, were not extensively and methodically recorded, when it was still possible to record them. The present work only preserves a pittance of the once opulent treasury of song.

For most of the millennium during which Goan Song was presumably in existence, it followed the musical style of *monophony* – traditional in Indian music, both classical and folk – which employs a single melodic line without accompaniment. We may assume that songs dealing with basic factors of Goan life and culture – as those referring to religion, childhood, death, occupations, theater and caste – were monophonic in character. Such songs, prevalent in Goa till at least the end of the 20th century, were in the 16th carried to the Dravidian lands of South Kanara and Kerala by Goan Hindu emigrants fleeing from the Inquisition, which had been established in 1556. It is possible that the Konkani songs that survive in these lands – where the linguistic, literary and musical traditions are so different from the Konkani – may have preserved the characteristics of the Goan music of the 16th century: their study would thus be invaluable for appreciating the development of Goan Song.

With the arrival of the Portuguese in Goa in the early 16th century, Konkani music was confronted with a new musical style, Western European in origin, employing *harmony*, where usually three or more sounds combine simultaneously to form a chord: if there is a plurality of chords, they are all interrelated. It took time for harmony to modify Goan music, for harmonized Goan songs do not appear to have been composed before the 18th century: they include Christian hymns and perhaps songs for folk plays.

In the early 19th century (from around 1830, to be precise), Goan music was impacted by another characteristically Western cultural phenomenon – social or ballroom dancing – that was to affect that music deeply and to inspire the creation of the epitome of Goan Song, the Mando. Goan architecture, as it was being developed at that stage, also favored the practice of dance. In the vast mansions built by the aristocrats, a large hall, the ballroom, was reserved for festive occasions, the high point of which was the dance. Goans became addicted to ballroom dancing: they mastered the dances of the 18th century (the Minuet and the Contredanse, which combine in a kind of synthesis in the Mando); and of the 19th century (like the Lanciers, a variety of the Contredanse, the Mazurka, the Polka and the Waltz; as well as the Pas-de-Quatre, invented in France in 1892). Goan dancers and singers now required their Konkani songs to have melodies that could direct and accompany ballroom dancing. Besides the Mando – and performed subsequent to it – were three other dance-song types, the Mando-Dulpod, the Dulpod and the Deknni.

A brief description of these four types follows. The *Mando* is a slow verse-and-refrain song, in six-four time, dealing with love, tragedy and contemporary events, both social and political. The *Mando-Dulpod* is a slower variety of the Dulpod (or a quicker sort of Mando), also in six-four time, facilitating the transition from the slow rhythm of the Mando to the quicker one of the Dulpod. The *Dulpod* itself, in six-eight time, is typically descriptive of everyday Goan life, particularly that of the Christians. The *Deknni* ("song of the Deccan" or "in the Deccani style"?) is a song imitating Hindu music in the musical idiom current among the Christians, in two-four or six-eight time, descriptive mostly of Hindu life, with special attention paid to the temple dancers. This volume is devoted to two of these types that follow and accompany the Mando.

The last three types have not been widely studied. The pioneer collector of Konkani folk songs, MIGUEL VICENTE DE ABREU (1827-1884), concentrated on the Dulpod; from 1866 to 1870, he collected many samples of the type ["Um Curioso", *Ramalhetinho de alguns hymnos e canções profanas em portuguez e concani offerecidas a mocidade goana de ambos os sexos*. Nova Goa: Imprensa Nacional, fasc.1 (1866), fasc. 2 (1870)]. Abreu's collection was made while dulpods were still being composed; the present collection was completed when their period of composition had long ended. They portray an idyllic world that in our own lifetime has vanished past recall, and which some of us were privileged to witness while it still enjoyed some of its vitality. Among the types portrayed here are the *advogad* (lawyer), *alfiad (alfaiate,* tailor), *beatinny* (pious spinster), *bikari* (beggar), *firngi (paklo,* white man, particularly a Portuguese), *forvoti* (sawyer), *harvi* (fisherman), *iscrivaum* (scrivener, notary), *inglez* (Englishman), *kolvont* (temple dancer), *marinheir* (seaman), *maskany* (really *masollykany,* fishwife), *mistis* (mestizo), *padri (padre vigar,* vicar, *padre cur,* curate, *patiu,* priest, *from padre-tio,* uncle priest), *poskar* and *poskany* (from *posorkar,* shop owner, merchant, male and female), *render* (toddy tapper), *rendenny* (toddy tapper's wife), *roper* (clothier), *sonar* (goldsmith), *tanddel* (ferryman) and *tovoi mest* (carpenter).

Not many folklorists have analyzed the Dulpod. Among

the few who have are ANTÓNIO MASCARENHAS (1916-1993) and LÚCIO RODRIGUES (1915-1973), particularly the latter, who not inaptly termed it "the song of joy". For it describes the life of Goa, such as it was lived in the 19th century and in the first half of the 20th, with joy and enthusiasm: this stands in contrast to the way some Goan writers in Portuguese viewed that life, like the novelist "GIP" (FRANCISCO JOÃO DA COSTA, 1864-1901) and the short story writer JOSÉ DA SILVA COELHO (1889-1944). Both saw it as a tissue of hypocrisy and pretense, features which it undoubtedly possessed. The Dulpod, however, depicts the other side of that life, as authentic as the one portrayed by the satirists.

Helpful in dating the dulpods are political events to which they sometimes allude, like the rebellion of Kuxttoba (1869), the Abkary Act (1878), the building of the railway (1881-1886) and the revolt of the Rannos (1895). The songs are for the most part anonymous. But occasionally we have been able to trace the name of the composers, like AZAVEDO DINIZ (1860-1907), ARNALDO DE MENEZES (1863-1917), CARMO ABREU (fl.1887-1894), FRANCISCO MENEZES (fl.1906-1910), GIZELINO REBELO (1875-1931), MEST FILIP (fl. early 20th cent.) and PAULO MILAGRES SILVA (1855-1931). Not all the verses of the songs attributed to them are necessarily theirs, however; the Dulpod is a folk song, and as such was subject to variation, accretion, and improvisation.

The songs printed here were collected with care and from several sources, but these sources are not indicated in this book. (Among them are the notebooks of my dear departed friend MICAEL MARTINS, 1914-1999.) The proper place to list them is a critical edition of dulpods, which would contain not only the critical apparatus, but also the score, a translation, and a commentary on some of the individual songs. This volume limits itself to score, text, and translation.

These songs were mainly composed in *Saxtty* /Salcete in villages like Bannali/Benaulim, Kurhtori/Curtorim, Kutthal/Cortalim, Lotlli/Loutulim, Makzon/Macazana, Morhgoum/Margão, Murgoum/Mormugão, Naveli/Navelim, Rai/Raia, São Tomé, Sankvall/Sancoale, Surali/Seraulim, and Tsandor/Chandor. Among other Saxtty villages whose names appear are Kunkol-lli/Cuncolim and Vel-lli/Velim.

Some other provinces, towns and villages in Goa mentioned are *Tisvarh* or Ilhas (Divarhi/Divar, Dongri, Malar, Ponnji, Raibondar/Ribandar); *Antruz* (Fonddem/Ponda, Kunddoi/Cundaim, Xirvoddem/Siroda); *Bardez* (Asgoum/Assagão, Kongotti/Calangute, Mapxem/Mapuça Pomburpem/Pomburpa, Porri/Parra, Xiuli/Siolim); and the Goan hinterland (Kalem, Narvem, Sonallem).

The dialect of the Dulpod (and the Deknni) is mainly Bambonn Saxtti (Salcetan as spoken by the Brahmins). In Saxtty, as in other parts of the Konkan, the dialect has caste variations. In the dulpods even members of other castes, like the *renders* (toddy tappers), for instance, adopt the speech of the Brahmins; but other caste forms are sometimes mixed with those of Brahmins. Seldom are non-Brahmin forms used consistently in any particular song.

Frequently, in public performances and private, the speech of the dulpods is changed into Barhdexi, on the mistaken assumption that the latter is the standard form of Konkani. Even if that were the case, it is evident that a song is best sung in the manner in which it was composed. It is true that there is (or was) a Standard Konkani (*Pramann Konkanni*], that was prevalent in the 16th and 17th centuries, but it was not Barhdexi (which evolved later and developed some sort of literature only in the 19th century, and whose contribution to Goan Song is, incidentally, small).

The Deknni's portrayal of Hindu ways shows the Goan Christian's nostalgia for a lost past, but also a sense of amusement at the strange habits of the people living on the other side of the Zuari river, in the shadow of their domed temples.

As noted above, the upper class Goans learnt social dancing around 1830, and the first mandos appear a little after that date. The deknni *Kuxttoba* seems to have been composed four decades later, for it was in 1869 that a guerilla chief of that name was defying the government and terrorizing the people. If the Deknni was not created at that time, it must have acquired its present shape through an adaptation of an old song type to the movements of the social dance. Indeed, in 1585, the Third Provincial Council of Goa had decreed that women were not to learn to dance, play, or sing *deqhanins*, which may well have been predecessors of our Deknni. Pieces like the *Altorhi Gonga* and the *Aj somaratso disu*, which seem to have vestiges of old Indian music, point to the plausibility of the latter theory.

As has been noted, the Deknni's main subjects are Hindu temples, partly concealed in the shadows of the Goan jungles, and the people who worship and work in them. There are no descriptions of the sacred buildings, but in one instance the poet pictures the colorful little items of the ceremonial – tiny heaps of lampblack and vermilion, water sparkling like jewels and a stool encrusted with gems (see *Kazoll kukumm mannyka' pannim*). But another deknni refers to the mundane side of temple life: a temple servant is reminded that the floor of his shrine needs to be swept.

Of the people in temple life, the dancers (or *kolvonts*) stand out: indeed, they are the Deknni's star actresses. They have names like Boiru, Dulgem, Mogrem and Sundorem. Their looks are seldom portrayed; more attention is given to what they wear. Like all Konkani girls they love to have flowers in their hair, and they flaunt their anklets (*painzonnam*) and nose-rings (*notim*), which become almost their distinctive marks. Some deknnis also tell us of their food habits. They eat a hash of spiced greens (*xaky baji*), with *tendllim* and cucumbers as added savories. They are said to have betel leaf and nut for breakfast, and butter and ghee for lunch. Other deknnis suggest that their job is to worship the god in the shrine, sometimes at night, to see if he runs away (see *Fulo mallunum)*. Besides, they have to dance a lot and allow themselves to be made love to. They dance for the village chief (*desai*) of Fonddem/Ponda and others of his kind, wiggling their hips to the tune of the cornet; and also at weddings, in getting to which they have to cross a river (see *Aum saiba peltorhi voitam*) in the canoe of an amorous ferryman. Him they try to persuade to take them into his boat by making presents of their ornaments, which the man makes a fuss of refusing (see *Ge ge ge ge ge*). Some of these women are met with on hills, beside the rippling water; others live on the sacred mountain (or Porvot) of Chandranath, near Pad-ddem/Paroda. Coming down from the mountain to the plains, they lose their way; a man takes them home with him (see *Amim kolvontam*). The dallying between the lovers is often a kind of game, where the dancer pretends that she has lost the flowers and jewelry on her head, nose, neck, hands, and feet, the man pointing out that each ornament is still where it is supposed to be (see *Muzo fulantso porhu*).

Some of these men are portrayed as great womanizers. One deknni tells of a man going without food to save his rupee to pay a woman for her services, and another of a man so infatuated by the courtesan Boiru that he gives the girl a third of his property and offers to support her over and above it (see *Satti ozranch'm bens*). An eager philanderer is the temple servant (*deulli*) who serves the Brahmin priest (*bott, bhatt*), who serves the gods. The *bott* dies and becomes ash, his wife dies and becomes mud (see *Bottu melo*). The most popular among the gods is Gonnes or Gonnespoti (Ganapati). Garlands of leaves deck the devotee's house for this god's banquet. Bands play, and devotional songs are sung before his image illuminated by oil lamps. Small packets of betel leaf are placed in front of the idol. He remains in the house for a month and then, preceded by a procession of temple dancers, he is carried to a well (or river) and tipped into it (see *Gonnespoti raya*, by Arnaldo de Menezes).

Besides such month-long devotions, there are ceremonies limited to particular days, such as Monday, when worshipers fall prostrate before the idol (see *Ag' y aga sonar xetti*). On such days too, weddings are celebrated, like those of the goldsmith caste, announced by the thump of the *murdong* (*mridanga*) drums. Not only caste weddings, but also caste activities, interest the composers of the Deknni. The goldsmith is described as making an ornament shaped like a forest- or wild- fig flowers. There is the cowherd (*gounlli*) from the hills, whose cows give a rich milk that is the delight of visitors (see *Kazoll kukumm mannyka' pannim*). The lowest caste is that of the *mar/mhar*; its members live in abandoned houses and make baskets out of sliced bamboo strips. From low caste the deknni shoots up to the eminence of the *Ray*, the king, perhaps the Kadamba king, known in popular legend as Kuzmo or Kozmu Ray, member of a dynasty which ruled Goa from after the 6th to the middle of the 13th century (see *Saiba rayan bandu gatila*).

The Deknni can never stay for long in one place. From colorful and sentimental historical events it hops to the familiar, quickly touching on several subjects – mother slicing an onion, a girl washing a copper pot and plates, and the quarrels between mother-in-law and daughter-in-law. It talks of the flirts of Xirvorhem/Siroda, who leave their windows open at night. It pries into clandestine love affairs. A man one morning succeeds in ravishing his mate's girl (*cherhum cumparilem*), and a young aristocrat of the Kon'jem/ Corjem ward of Kurhtori is caught going to the Xirvorhem temple for the *kolvonts*.

The latter instance is taken from the life of the Christian districts, which the Deknni (like the Mando) depicts best when it portrays the bride, who in one case is so rich that the poet resorts to onomatopoeia (*sonnom sonnom sonnom sonnom sa* !) to echo the jingle of this Lakshmi's surplus of coins. Christian also are the two extraordinary characters Henriqueta and Adelaide, who must have been real people, as must also the Portuguese card player "Cuxuxu". Foreigners do not often intrude into the Deknni's closed world. One song tells of a Portuguese who comes from his country with only eighteen rupees, and another tells of the English who build a railway from Bombay to Poona, and from across the Ghats into Goa, which will shatter the tranquil world of the latter for good.

An undoubted historical figure is Kuxttoba, the guerilla Ranno (forester, hillman), "heir of India and terror of Goa", who became a hero notwithstanding his terrible raids on the countryside. A *bott* who spied for the Portuguese government raped a woman of Kuxttoba's family. Vowing revenge, the fiery Ranno rebelled, and kept the government troops at bay, until he was betrayed and put to death in 1871. There is a deknni, *Kuxttoba,* which narrates in a detailed jumble of fact and legend of his killing of the *bott*, and of his incarceration in the Arsenal of Velha Goa before his rebellion of 1868.

Nostalgically evoked is the Hindu past - of Krishna's *gokula* (the village where the god spent his bucolic boyhood) and of anklets tinkling on the banks of the Ganga and Yamuna at the old Prayaga, the confluence of the two sacred streams. The lady's nose-ring is lost, and she implores her husband to find it (see *Altorhi Gonga*). The songs on Kuxttoba and on the sacred rivers show the Deknni's serious and romantic side, and are perhaps its finest achievement.

Besides the description to the meteoric rise and eclipse of Kuxttoba, another historical episode is found described in the deknnis, the building of the railway by the British in 1886. This event, which prefigured the coming of industrialism, deformed the pattern of Goan life and upset its traditional balance definitively. The lure of money took everyone away from the fields, even young girls, some of whom became promiscuous. The same deknni that tells this story alludes to one of the many Ranno uprisings against the Portuguese that occurred at this time. These and other factors, like the mention of coins (*rubo, tanga*, etc.), which went out of use after the arrival of the rupees-annas-pies currency, are also of great help in dating the deknnis.

Descriptions of animals and plants form the Deknni's most charming and picturesque side. Monkeys frisk on trees, jackal pups lie at the foot of a wild fig tree, and a tiger kills a cow on an evening. Inlaid in this side's surface are gem-like descriptions of the weddings of the vegetables and fishes, which show the Deknni at its most colorful. The plump purple eggplant is to wed; at this the chili turns fiery red with anger and envy, the twisted snake gourd turns up its nose in disgust, and the fat pumpkin slumps into a round ball of resignation. This is the complicated figure of speech of Sanskrit poetics, the *aprastutaprasamsa* – the conveying of the poem's subject matter, like the wedding of humans, by that which is not the subject matter, like a collection of fruits and vegetables that have metaphorical similarities to those humans (see *Vaingem cazar zata munn*). At the marriage of the fishes the tortoise sings a song in the water, while the fox does a dance on the bank. It is significant that the deknni that recounts this opens on the proclamation of the lord king, the *Ray*. A dim historical memory (of long forgotten Hindu kings) livens with nostalgia, *saudade*, persisting in the melancholy of the music even when the text goes on to allude to funny things (like the antics of animals on the river bank. See *Saiba rayan bandu gatila*).

Much of the fascination of the Deknni lies in this haunting music, which, as much as any other factor, determines the grouping of its themes. A melody, originally composed for one set of words, is borrowed by another (often quite different in content from the first text) resulting in a cluster of parasites around the original nucleus. In our edition, the chunks of homogeneous texts are indicated by Roman numerals (also used to indicate broad divisions within a deknni).

It was in the dance halls of the aristocrats' manors of Saxtty that the Deknni arose, and where, on festive occasions, its songs were improvised. Arnaldo de Menezes himself tried his hand at one, to commemorate one of the pranks that he and his friends (among others, Azavedo Diniz and Aleixo António Costa) played on the village goldsmith, Ori (Hari). Without anyone's knowledge they fixed a net in a well into which, after his devotions, Ori threw his clay image of the elephant-faced god, Ganapati. Not long after the wicked boys took the image out of the net and placed it outside the goldsmith's door, which caused Ori no little consternation when he discovered it. This occurred at Kurhtori. Of all places in Goa, Xirvorhem – village of temples, dancers, and music, opposite to Kurhtori – comes into the Deknni most often. Kurhtori itself is referred to twice: in the deknni *Satti ozranch'm bens* a young aristocrat from Batt (*battantulo bab*), on the banks of the Zuari, is seen going to Mannkem, a ferry to Xirvorhem on the opposite bank. In *Erekity Adelai-i*, the suitors in long robes are asked to wait on *Diogitso band* (Diogi's bund, Yogis' bund?) which is off the same river. In the same deknni there is also reference to the neighboring village of Rai/Raia. Fonddem is mentioned several times; so is Bori/Borim, the village in Antruz, which had the ferry (now spanned by a bridge) on the road to Fonddem. Murgoum/Mormugão, the tongue-like thrust of Saxtty into the sea, appears once. To the north is the island of Tisvarh/one of the Ilhas, containing the city of Velha Goa. The roads to that old metropolis are fringed with zigzagging ridges of fields, and were once trodden by Kuxttoba's manacled feet. To the south, towering over Saxtty, is the mountain sacred to the

Moon Lord Chandranatha, wooded on its sides and crowned by the domed temple to the moon – a vision of a phantasmal white fane over jungle of green which can stand as a symbol of a poetry dreamily evoking a distant past while entangled in a wild fantasy of the odd and the sensual, which is what the Deknni is.

* * *

Note: The text and score of the Deknnis is basically the same as was published in José Pereira & Micael Martins, *A Sheaf of Deknnis*. Bombay: The Konkan Cultural Association, 1967. This work also contains a list of sources, of the text and score: manuscripts and informants who have all since passed away.

ACKNOWLEDGMENTS

We are deeply grateful to our friends, Victor Rangel Ribeiro, for his perceptive editorial comments, and Álvaro Peres da Costa, for procuring for us the sponsorship of Goan Overseas Association of New South Wales, Australia.

TEXT, SCORE, TRANSLATION AND NOTES

Mando-Dulpods

1. ADVOGADANY'M VARHOILEAIM HARHAM
2. AITRACH' SOKANNIM MISSAKO
3. BANNALEANTUM MUZO GAUM-UM
4. CECILIO MUJEM NAUM
5. DANDDEA' CAETAN BUTIQUEIRU
6. ESTUD SANDDUN BOUNTAM MUNN
7. GARANTULIM BAIRI SOT-TONNOM
8. IM TIM LOTLLE' BAMBONNAM
9. LANOM Y AUM BURGEM ASTONNOM
10. *Carmo Abreu & Arnaldo de Menezes,* MAIM-PAI MAKA KORYTAI RE FUGARO
11. RAINTUM TSOLI DINAIM KONNOM
12. SANGEARY AUM [SANKVALLE] PARHUM' GELOLIM
13. *Arnaldo de Menezes,* TAMBRHEM NESUN FOTO

Mando-Dulpod **1**

ADVOGADANY'M VARHOILEAIM HARHAM

1. Advogadany'm varhoileaim harham
   Galnum bountai sobrecazacam
   Atam' tankam dorum' kolnnaim penam
   E rerheam' konny'm dileaim cartam

2. Oido pichea' xikileai-i soro
   Letrado bountai goro-dero
   Durhuvancheo geunum raxi
   E letrad cauzo galtai fatti

3. Putanum carto kal-llam munnum
   Maim-im sogli natsota
   Da ozar doti magota
   Vistidachi sunom at-ttoly' muntta

1. The lawyers have grown long beards. They go around wearing waistcoats. They don't know how to hold their pens in their hands. Who gave these idiots (lit. buffaloes) lawyers' diplomas ?

2. The doctors have learnt to drink. Lawyers go from door to door. Making a pile of money these lawyers delay their cases.

3. Now that her son has got a diploma, mother is all excited (lit. is all dancing). She is asking ten thousand (rupees) as dowry. She says she will get a daughter-in-law who wears a dress [a Westernized girl, as opposed to a wearer of the native *torhop-baz*].

Mando-Dulpod 2

AITRACH' SOKANNIM MIŠSAKO

pa - su man-num fal - so Mes-tri re - bec za - nnom
cum - pas ne - nnom A - men a - men a - men Mes - tri re - bec za - nnom
cum - pas ne - nnom A - men a - men a - men Rag ta - ka ai -
lo So - kanny'm ye - nas - to - nnom rau - lo Rag ta - ka ai -
lo So - kanny'm ye - nas - to - nnom rau - lo A - tam san - je ai - la
re U - grha - su kon - num ful - llo A - tam san - je ai - la
re U - grha - su kon - num ful - llo Mes - tri re - bec za - nnom
cum - pas ne - nnom A - men a - men a - men Mes - tri re - bec za - nnom
cum - pas ne - nnom A - men a - men a - men
D.C.

1. Aitrach' sokannim missako
   Mestri vajita valso
   Mestri rebec vajit' re
   Cumpasu man-num falso

2. Rag taka y ailo
   Sokanny'm yenastonnom raulo
   Atam sanje y aila re
   Ugrhasu kon-num ful-llo

3. Devan dilam taka tsorho
   Tem korum' bounta vorho
   Amim sogott magtai re
   Devan korum' tujem goro

   COR: Mestri rebec zannom, cumpas nennom
   Y amen y amen y amen

1. At mass on Sunday morning, the choirmaster plays a waltz. Choirmaster plays on a violin, keeping the wrong time.
2. He was annoyed and did not come in the morning. He has come now in the evening remembering what happened earlier (or his previous appointment).
3. God has given him much, and he is working to increase it. We are all praying that God make him prosper (*lit.* make his home).

   Chorus: Choirmaster knows (how to play) the violin, but not how to keep time. Amen, amen, amen!

Mando-Dulpod 3

BANNALEANTUM MUZO GAUM-UM

1. Bannaleantum muzo gaum-um
   Aulako otam y aum-um
   Eku tsampeantso purho geun ge cumary
   Ogrhailem naum-om

2. Estudako otonnom
   Bollsant bolu galnum velo
   Mogu axilolo dekun cumarik
   Soglo havoilo

3. Rubachi nam re zorhi
   Sukunum zalea mori
   Eki cumari maka mel-lli ga saiba
   Hapri pitolli

4. Dispidiro tuka kelem
   Aulako yenam munnum
   Cumarinum apoicha' dal-llo re tuka
   Cazara' lagunum

1. Bannali/Benaulim is my village. I attend school. I disgraced myself, my dear girl, with a bouquet of champak flowers (that I gave you).

2. On my way to school (to study), I took a cake in my pocket. Because I was in love I fed all of it to my girl friend.

3. I don't have a dime (two pennies, or *rubos*). The girl has grown as thin as an eel (*mori* fish). I met a dark girl friend, sir, as pretty as a bird (*hapri pitolly*, paradise flycatcher?).

4. I said goodbye to you, because you don't come to school. Your girl friend sent for you, my boy, because of the wedding.

Mando-Dulpod 4

CECILIO MUJEM NAUM

I

CECILIA 1. Cecilio mujem naum
Moga moga cherhum curiozo y aum

CUMPARY 2. Tum curiozo zaleari
Talhar kon-num darhi maka judi

CECILIA 3. Talhar korunko judi
Moga moga burgi muji moti

II

CUMPARY 4. Tum curiozo zaleari
Bordar kon-num fronhi di go tori

CECILIA 5. Aum fronhi ditam tuka
Utrachi mudi di re maka

CUMPARY 6. Utrach' mudi diucha' tuka
Mainchem muje licens zai go maka

III

CUMPARY 7. Papak pagment porhche furhem
Cecily' tum kon-num darhy go virhio

8. Papan dal-llam kaporho
Cecily' tum lambo sorhy go mirio

9. Undiro mat-tai urhio
Cecily' tum damun dory go mirio

10. Cumparinum dal-llam pero
Cecily' tuka *quer ou não quer* -o

11. Cumparinum dal-llam cetim
Cecily' tum kon-num galy go tsollio

12. Sinaleko al-llea mudi
Cecily' tunvem pot-tun kitea dal-lli ?

IV

CUMPARY 13. Cecily' karhi maka dero
Uloucha' guttachi foboro

CECILIA 14. Aum-um karhy nam saiba dero
Mogacha marida' [poticha] bogoro

CUMPARY 15. Bailean sunneanchi bobatti
Cecily' tuka disonaka fotti

16. Cecily' karhy go matrech dero
    Uloichak guttachi foboro

17. Cecily' maka konnom nam sangati
    Dovory maka ekech punnum rati

18. To putu majoralo
    Cecily' tunvem kon-num gexlo y aplo

CECILIA. 1. My name is Cecilia. Love, oh my love, I am a talented girl.

LOVER. 2. If you are talented, make me a jacket and send it to me.

CECILIA. 3. As to making a jacket, I am too young to know how to make it.

LOVER. 4. If you are talented, at least embroider a pillow-case for me.

CECILIA. 5. I will give you a pillow-case; give me an engagement ring.

LOVER. 6. To give you an engagement ring, I need mother's permission.

7. Before your father gets paid, Cecilia make me some cigarettes and send them to me.

8. Father has sent you a sari. (When you wear it) leave large folds.

9. The mice are jumping. Cecilia, keep your folds close together.

10. Your lover has sent you a guava, Cecilia, do you want it or not?

11. Your lover has sent you a piece of satin. Make a blouse, Cecilia, and wear it.

12. I have brought you a ring as a sign (of my commitment to marry you). Cecilia, why did you return it?

13. Cecilia, open the door for me. So we can talk our secret (lovers') talk.

CECILIA. 14. I will not open the door to you sir, without my husband (being near).

LOVER. 15. The dogs are barking outside. This is no trick Cecilia.

16. Please open the door Cecilia, so we can talk our secret lovers' talk.

17. I have no companion, Cecilia. Take me in for one night at least.

18. He is the son of a major. Cecilia, you acquired him for yourself.

Mando-Dulpod 5

DANDDEA' CAETAN BUTIQUEIRU

1. Danddea' Caetan butiqueiru
To zoborh fitixeiru
Tea Jaquina baie
Beiju diucha' ota
Ubo man-num feru

2. Donim-tinim muinnem zale
Jaquin vareako geleari
Tum kosolem varem
Geta go Jaquin
Bannalê' velleri

3. Naveleche munn te burge
Amche kot-tai-i moskore
Caetan baba' sangunum
Tanche menddeanche
Karhum' laitoly'm dolle

COR: Ai, ai, Jaquin baienum
Kandonnanim dilo takam maru

1. Danddea' Caetano the shopkeeper is a real rogue. He runs straight to Miss Joaquina to give her a kiss.

2. Two or three months have passed since Joaquina went to the seashore for the air. What kind of air are you taking, Joaquina, on the beach at Bannali/Benaulim?

3. Those Naveli boys are making fun of us. I'll tell Mr. Caetano and make him tear out their eyes.

Chorus: Oh, oh, Miss Joaquina beat them with rice pounders.

Mando-Dulpod 6

ESTUD SANDDUN BOUNTAM MUNN

1. Estud sanddun bountam munn
   Tuka sangilolem konnem
   Anim carto y anvem kal-llam go Leonor
   Juridic xikuch' furhem

2. Pai-i tuzo mon-num go
   Tuka zai toxem zalem
   Anim zai-i toxem kon-num go Leonor
   Naum-om perder kelem

1. Who told you Leonor, that I have given up my studies and am wandering about? Leonor, I got my lawyer's diploma even before I had studied law!

2. When your father died, my girl, everything happened as you wished (you did what you liked). And when everything had gone your way you besmirched your name.

Mando-Dulpod 7

GARANTULIM BAIRI SOT-TONNOM

1. Garantulim bairi sot-tonnom
   Umbra' y ad-ddun dun-niri pol-llim

2. Umbra' y ad-ddun dun-niri pol-llim
   Donim atim' kanknnam fol-llim

3. Sanje muzo poti ietolo
   Donim atim' kanknnam soitolo

4. Eku valar aileari [eileari] puro
   Donim atim' kanknnam souchako

5. Durhu naxleary bato ditolo
   Donim atim' kanknnam soitolo

6. Aga muja valar mama
   Donim atim' kanknnam soi ga

1. As I was leaving the house, I knocked against the threshold and fell.

2. I knocked against the threshold and fell. I broke the bangles of my two hands.

3. My husband will come in the evening, and have bangles fitted on my two hands.
4. I hope a bangle seller will come to fit the bangles on my two hands.
5. If my husband has no money, he will give (the bangle seller) paddy. He will have bangles fitted on my two hands.
6. Oh my bangle seller, sir, please fit the bangles on my two hands.

Mando-Dulpod 8

IM TIM LOTLLE' BAMBONNAM

Im tim Lotllê' bambonnam
Matea' malttai-i kandollam
O to menddo patrat pinjit re
Sanjê nastonnam

Those Lotlli/Loutulim Brahmins wear *kandollam* flowers in their hair. This rogue boasts while he has nothing for the evening.

Kandollam, Aegicerus maius, has fragrant flowers.

Mando-Dulpod 9

LANOM Y AUM BURGEM ASTONNOM

1. Lanom y aum burgem astonnom
   Paiko-mainko vely'm Devanum
   Atam y anvem sangat sodila
   Caetan babu Devanum nirmila

2. Delicad tsomkonn go tujem
   Caetan baba' monam' gelem
   Posgem aum firngeache kulliechem
   Juzefin naum mum re mujem

3. Zoborh mog bariku finum
   Jeulom' jevonn vosnam jin-num
   Tuzo maca ugrhasu aileary re
   Ratich'm mujem pott yeta fulunum

   COR: Tsoi, tsoi, tsoi
   Xiunteam' porh matea malttolem
   Magiry aum tumgery re yetolem

1. When I was a little girl, God took away my father and mother. Now I have sought a companion. God destined Mr. Caetano for me.

2. Your delicate gait went to Mr. Caetano's head. I am an orphan, Portuguese by race. Josefina is my name.

3. My love is fine and delicate (so much so that) I cannot digest my food. At night when I think of you, my stomach swells (I am filled with happiness).

Chorus: Look, look and see. I will wear a garland of chrysanthemums on my head and come to visit you.

Carmo Abreu & Arnaldo de Menezes

Mando-Dulpod **10**

MAIM-PAI MAKA KORYTAI RE FUGARO *

Maim-pai maka korytai re fugaro
Uksar baie zau munttai cazaro
Gor-der mugely'm tukach voro
Begim bai tum zau-u go cazaro

My father and mother are nagging me; "get married soon," they are saying. "Take my house and all for yourself, but do get married, my girl."

* Improvised around the time of the wedding (1894), alluded to in the dulpod, of José Pereira's grandmother, Arcângela da Piedade ("Lucrécia") Menezes (1875-1951) and grandfather Mateus Francisco Pereira (1875-1949).

Mando-Dulpod 11

RAINTUM TSOLI DINAIM KONNOM

1. Raintum tsoli dinaim konnom
   Em soglem bembreanchem gamponnom
   Raintum tsoli dinaim munnum
   Randdam' sodum' bountai-i aponnom

2. Raiturkaram' nam re zati
   Arham sukun lagnaim tanche kati'
   Aponn confradi munnchako
   Geunum bountai Bom Jesuchi vati

1. No one in Rai/Raia gives (any of those men) his daughter to wed. We have here a bunch of sniveling idiots (snotty guys). As no father in Rai gives them his daughter, they go about looking for widows.

2. The men of Raitur/Rachol have no honor (lit. caste); their bones, gone dry, do not stick to their skin. To call themselves confrères, they go around holding candles from the Bom Jesus (church).

Mando-Dulpod 12

SANGEARY AUM [SANKVALLE] PARHUM' GELOLIM

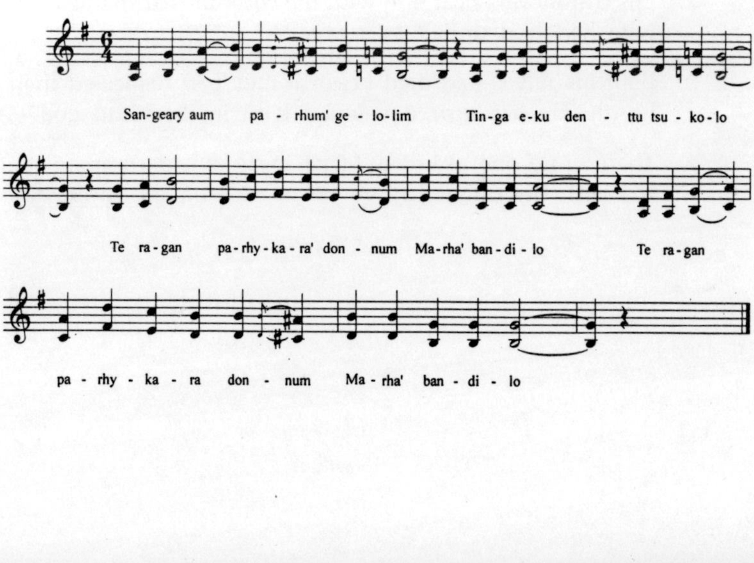

1. Sangeary aum [Sankvalle] parhum' gelolim
   Tinga eku denttu tsukolo
   Te ragan parhykara' don-num
   Marha' bandilo

2. Baraborcha parhykaranim
   Rorho taka dilo xeukanim
      [Maru taka galo xeukanim]
   Bailen taka son-nnum al-llo ga
   Upkaranim

3. Dogeo tajo bailo meleo
   Cuidad tankam nam zaun jivatso
   Atam taka bavarht rigola
   Kud-ddea devatso

4. Garantum naim-im konnom
   Bailean [Bailam'] bitory zatai-i narhi
   Papan muja bokrho angoila
   Porvotari

1. I went to Sangem (Sanguem)/Sankvall (Sancoale) to harvest coconuts. There a coconut scoop was missed. Angry at that, they tied the plucker to the coconut tree.
2. His co-pluckers beat him with the coconut tree spathes. His wife had him untied as a favor.
3. Both his wives had died because they had neglected their health. He has now developed faith in the blind god.
4. There is no one at home. Strife rages outside (among the women). My father has vowed a cock on the Mountain.

Arnaldo de Menezes

Mando-Dulpod 13

TAMBRHEM NESUN FOTO

Tambrhem nesun foto
Bendda' bandil' tonnantso ventto
Dogeoi naikinny' salam' galtai
Chiny'lam' kottkotto

They wear a red ceremonial *torhop* , (and to keep it on) they have tied it with a rope of straw. The two "princesses" are dancing in the hall, making a tap-tap with their sandals.

Deknnis

1. AG' Y AGA SONAR XETTI
   Variant 1. ARE ARE XETTI DADA
   Variant 2. BAVACH' BOINNIM
2. AJ SOMARATSO DISU
   Variant. AMCHA SOMARACHA DISA
3. ALTORHI GONGA
4. ALTORHY SAN PELTORHI GELEARI
5. AMIM KOLVONTAM
6. ARE DEULLEA (no score)
7. AT-LAUNNEM ZALEM DADA
8. AUM SAIBA PELTORHI VOITAM
9. BOL-LOLY' XIDIE' MUKO NAM GA
10. BORIECHE TARI
11. BOTTU MELO
12. ERIKETY ADELAI-I (HENRIQUETA ADELAIDE)
13. ERIKETY BAÌ ADELAI-I (HENRIQUETA BAI ADELAIDE)
14. FARO DILE VO RE BABA
15. FONDDECHA DESIAGERY
16. FULO MALLUNUM
17. GE GE GE GE GE
18. *Arnaldo de Menezes,* GONNESPOTI RAYA
19. JAMNAM POROBAJA
20. KAINCH KARANN NAM
21. KAZOLL KUKUMM MANNYKA' PANNIM
22. KOLVONTAM Y AMIM PORVOTAVELIM
23. KUXTTOBA
24. MUJI MAIM-IM BOISOLEA
25. MUZO FULANTSO PORHU
   Variant 1. MUJEM PAIANCHEM PAINZONN
   Variant 2. MUZO MOGATSO POTI
26. NAUM MUJEM ERIKETI (HENRIQUETA)
27. OIRY OIRY OIRY DOGRA'
28. PAIAM' PAINZONNAM

29. PONNJECHA PATTEARY MAIM
30. PORTUGALA' SAUN
31. SAIBA RAYAN BANDU GATILA
    Variant 1. AILE DONGURI
    Variant 2. SAIBA RAYANUM
32. SAIBA TANDDELA (no score)
33. SATTI OZRANCH' BENS MUJE ADINOM
34. SOKANNY'M FURHEM UTTUN CHERH'M MU'JM
35. TENDDULECHIM TENDDULIM
36. VAINGEM CAZAR ZATA MUNN
    Variant. VAINGEM CAZAR ZATA MUNN
37. VOKOL Y AMCHI LOKMI SORI
38. XIRVORHECHIM CHERHVAM

Deknni 1

AG' Y AGA SONAR XETTI

1. Ag' y aga sonar xetti
   Pettoi tujem agttem
   Ful zaundi zogtem dada
   Rumborhachem

2. Fulo rumborhachem dada
   Derhxam pakolleanchem
   Bavanum kon-num y aple
   Boinnim' diuchem

3. Arhy forem kudolly bava
Karhy eku depo
Tajery dovory rompo bava
Rumborhatso

4. Cazucha mullant bava
Y asai tego kole
Tantuly' dog don-num y arhxi
Zalea' polle

Papa-mamam Xerole
Cherh'm y aum binam binam!

1. Goldsmith, sir, light your brazier. Let your forest fig flower of gold sparkle.
2. The forest fig flower has a hundred and fifty petals. A brother should make it and give it to his sister.
3. Get your ax and pickax brother, unearth a clod, and put on it a sapling of the forest fig tree.
4. At the foot of the cashew tree there are three foxes, brother. See if you can catch two.

Chorus. Your father and mother are at Xeroli/Sirula, my girl! I have nothing to be afraid of, nothing to be afraid! [I can have my will on you.]

Deknni 1, Variant 1

ARE ARE XETTI DADA
Variant 1 of AG' Y AGA SONAR XETTI

COR 1: *Papa mamam dekinam*
Cherhva' biranti nam

1. *Are are xetti dada*
Pettoi tujem y agttem
Ful zaundi zogtem dada
Rumborhachem

2. *Bavache boinnim*
Bava' lagim zai tem tum mago
Rumbrhachem ful re dada
Darhi sango

3. *Kudolly munn ti man-num*
   Kud'lliry kal-llo depo
   Tajery dovory rompo dada
   Rumborhatso

COR 2: *Papa mamanche lojen*
   Cherh'm y aum binam binam

Deknni 1, Variant 2

BAVACH' BOINNIM
Variant 2 of AG' Y AGA SONAR XETTI

1. *Bavach' boinnim*
   Bava' lagim zai tem tum mago
   Rumborhachem fulo bava
   Darhi munn sango

2. *Rumbrhachem fulo bava*
   Derhxa pakolleanchem
   Bavanum kon-n y aple
   Boinnim' diuchem

3. *Rumbrhicha mullant dada*
   Teg rot-ttai kole
   Tantule dog don-num
   Arhxi polle

4. *Sonara dada muja*
Pettoi tujem y agttem
Kori zogtem fulo dada
Rumborhachem

5. *Kudolly man-num dada*
Karhi y eku depo
Taje' roi-i rompo dada
Rumborhatso

Deknni 2

AJ SOMARATSO DISU

1. Aj somaratso disu
Deva y at-paiem pot-ttai-i
Faro murdongi vaztai faro
Famm xettinge' lognank ga
Famm xettinge' lognanko

2. Aga desia muja mama
Tuka kolvont fuinchem zai-i
Mujem naum-om Sundory'm bai ga
Mujem naum-om Sundory'm bai-i

3. Y amy'm xaky-baji hatai-i
   Borxik tendduly'm anim touxim
   Y amim ganvan Xirvorhech'm ga
   Y amim ganvan Xirvorhechim

1. Today is Monday. They fall on their hands and feet before their god. Thumps resound on the earthenware drum. It is a signal for the goldsmiths' wedding, a signal of the goldsmiths' wedding.

2. Oh my uncle, desai, sir! Which of these dancing girls do you fancy?

DANCING GIRL: My name is Miss Sundorem, sir. My name is Miss Sundorem.

DANCING GIRLS. 3. We eat a mess of spiced vegetables, with *tendullim* and cucumbers for savories. We come from Xirvorhem/ Siroda, sir, we are Xirvorhem girls.

Verse 3, tenddulim. Known to botany as Cephalandra Indica *or* Momordica Monadelpha. *It is a smooth climber, with large flowers. The fruit, which is about 5 to 8 cm long, is red, and at first marked with white streaks.*

Deknni 2, Variant

AMCHA SOMARACHA DISA
Variant of AJ SOMARATSO DISU

1. *Amcha somaracha disa*
   Deva' at-paiem vollotati ga
   Deva' at-paiem vollotati
   Amcha xettingelea lognantum vo
   Amcha xettingelea lognantum
2. *Amim xaki baji hatati ga*
   Borxim tenddulim y anim touxim
   Amim ganvan Xirvorhechim ga
   Amim ganvan Xirvorhechim

Deknni 3

ALTORHI GONGA

1. Altorhi Gonga, poile torhi Jamnam
   Jazmi kakri ind' astonnam
   Nodre' diva nam

2. Aile torhi poile torhi painzonnam vazoti
   Mujem nakantulem noti
   Sanddlam
   Sodun di ga poti

1. On this bank is the Ganges, and on the other, the Yamuna. *And though the clear water flows down*, there is no lamp to my eyes.
2. On this bank and the other anklets tinkle. My nose ring, oh, my nose ring, has been lost! Find it for me please, my husband.

The meaning of the second line, shown in translation in italics, is unclear.

Deknni 4

ALTORHY SAN PELTORHI GELEARI

Altorhy san peltorhi geleari
Re makorh boisleai-i rukari
Ilo-ilo sor' galy mul-lleari
Re porhki kan-nn mal-li tokleari

Crossing from this bank of the river to the other I see monkeys sitting on the trees. I asked for a little, a tiny drop, of booze, and they flung the coconut-shell spoon on my head.

Dekmi 5

AMIM KOLVONTAM

1. Amim kolvontam
   Borieche tari
   Borieche tari dada
   Boriechi tari

2. Amgel' y almusu
   Panom-supari
   Panom-supari dada
   Panom-supari

3. Amgely'm jevonnom
   Tup y anim lonnim
   Tup y anim lonnim dada
   Tup y anim lonnim

1. We are dancing girls at the Bori/Borim ferry. At the Bori ferry, sir, at the Bori ferry.
2. Our breakfast is betel leaf and nut. Betel leaf and nut, sir, betel leaf and nut.
3. Our meal is butter and ghee. Butter and ghee sir, butter and ghee.

Deknni 6

ARE DEULLEA

Are deullea
Tuk' sangtam kannim
Tugelea deulla'
Marum' zai san-nnim

Temple servant, I'll tell you something (lit. a story). Your temple needs sweeping with a broom.

Deknni 7

AT-LAUNNEM ZALEM DADA

At-launnem zalem dada
At-launnem zalem
Mag direitu
Revezo magtam
Cuxuxu firngi
Faravola

Someone's been tapped on the shoulder, sir, tapped on the shoulder (lit, a touching of the hand has taken place). Ask for the direct dealing. I'll ask for a backstroke. Cuxuxu the white man is now in trouble.

The "tapping on the shoulder", "direct" and "contrary" dealing of cards are all terms of a card game which we have been unable to identify.

Deknni 8

AUM SAIBA PELTORHI VOITAM

1. Aum saiba peltorhi voitam
   Damulea lognank voitam

2. Paiantulim painzonn'm ditam
   Tariry voichi vatto dakoi

3. Atantuleo pattuleo ditam
   Tariry voichi vatto dakoi

4. Golleantuly' gollsory' ditam
   Tariry voichi vatto dakoi

5. Nakantuli noti ditam
   Tariry voichi vatto dakoi

Maka saiba vatto dakoi
Maka saiba vatto kollonam

Damulea mattvant kolvontantso fell/mell vo
Damulea mattvant kolvontantso fellu/mellu

1. I am going to the other bank, sir, I am going to Damu's wedding.
2. I will give you the anklets from my feet. Please show me the way to the ferry.
3. I will give you the bracelets from my wrists. Please show me the way to the ferry.
4. I will give you the necklace from my neck. Please show me the way to the ferry.
5. I will give you the ring from my nose. Please show me the way to the ferry.

> Show me the way to the ferry, please. I do not know the way
>
> In Damu's pavilion, there is a dance/meeting of the dancing girls.

Chorus: *"pavilion"* (mattou). *A structure, usually of bamboos, covered with leaves of coconut palm. It is erected on festive occasions, such as weddings and religious ceremonies, to shelter large numbers of people who cannot be accommodated in a residence or sacred building.*

Origin of the dekni's popularity. *"Aum saiba" is the best-known of the deknnis. The credit for popularizing it goes to Mestre Lourenço (Lourencinho) Henrique L. Dias, leader of the Banda Nacional de Salcete, who died around 1930. His band was in great demand at upper class weddings, especially for the "contredanses 'de honra'". "Aum saiba" was introduced as one of these "contredanses" at a wedding, probably that of Prazeres da Costa ("Musmbikar""the Mozambican"), in the early years of the 20th century, under the title "Bailados do Concão" (Dances of the Konkan). It was later published under that title by the composer Carlos Eugénio Ferreira at the Casa Rangel, Bastora, in 1926. The dekni's probable date is therefore the last decades of the 19th century.*

Deknni 9

BOL-LOLY' XIDIE' MUKO NAM GA

1. Bol-loly' xidie' muko nam ga
   Maim-im melea suniem' duko nam

2. Bol-loly' xidi xinkeari
   Maim-im melea' sun tintteari

3. Vatlleants' dall gansota
   Maim-im melea' sunom y ansota

4. Ganttary vot' konn mamie ge
   Tagelo zanvuim amim mum

1. A water-filled jar, sir, has no mouth. If the mother-in-law dies, the daughter-in-law does not grieve.

2. The filled pot is on the kitchen sling. If the mother-in-law dies, the daughter-in-law goes shopping (lit. is in the marketplace).

3. The pile of brass plates clatters merrily (is rubbed). When the mother-in-law dies, the daughter-in-law flutters happily (laughs).

4. Auntie, there is someone heading for the hills. His son-in-law, that's me.

Verse 2, kitchen sling (xinkem)*. A sling fixed to the roof, for keeping various kitchen utensils.*

Verse 3, brass plates (vatlli): dishes of brass or copper with steep sides, native to the region. Vatlli is the diminutive of vattem, a large tray-like dish.

Deknni 10

BORIECHE TARI

Borieche tari
Kolvontam darhi dada
Kolvontam darhi

Send the dancing girls to the Bori/Borim ferry, sir; send the dancing girls there.

Deknni 11

BOTTU MELO

I

1. Bottu melo
Botta' gobor zalo
Bottiny meli
Bottnim' mati zali

II

2. Seda' kaporho
Tsolliê' tambrhem chito
Kolvonto naum mujem
Pipirmitto

3. Naka' noti
Golleam' diamanti
Naka' noti
Golleam' diamanti

III

4. Bailo muji
Tontti, epran motti
Bailo muji
Tontti, epran motti

IV

5. Ol-lli xemainchi
Kamai kedi
Ol-lli xemainchi
Kamai kedi

V

6. Ruban ditai ti
Goinchi xidi
Ruban ditai ti
Goinchi xidi

7. Ruban ditai to
Konkonn dudi
Ruban ditai to
Konkonn dudi

1. The Brahmin priest died, and he became ash. The Brahminee died – she became mud.
2. A sari of silk, a bodice of red calico. I am a dancing girl, and my name is Lozenge (Peppermint).
3. A ring on my nose, diamonds on my neck. A ring on my nose and diamonds on my neck.
4. My wife is lame, but expert in business. My wife is lame, but expert in business.
5. How clever my grandmother is, how clever she is!
6. They are selling Goan water pots for a *rubo* each. They are selling Goan water pots for a *rubo* each.
7. They are selling white pumpkins for a *rubo* each. They are selling white pumpkins for a *rubo* each.

Deknni 12

ERIKETY ADELAI-I (HENRIQUETA ADELAIDE)

Erekity Adelai-i
Dogaintsoi pai-i cumpari
Vaganum mal-li ga
Kaly sanjechi gai-i

Dad is godfather to both Henriqueta and Adelaide. The tiger/ leopard, sir, killed yester evening's cow.

Deknni 13

ERIKETY BAI ADELAI-I (HENRIQUETA BAI ADELAIDE)

1. Erikety bai Adelai-i
   Dogaintso pai-i cumpari
   Vaganom kaly mal-li gai-i
   Sokannim yeta vai-i

2. Bai muji bai-i
    Kaly geli Rai-i
    Ailole voulle
    Galtai kabai-i
    Diogich' bandary
    Rabai-i

1. Misses Henriqueta and Adelaide – daddy is godfather to them both. The tiger killed the cow yesterday. The stench comes in the morning.

2. My dear daughter went yesterday to Rai/Raia. All the suitors who turn up wear long frocks. All of you wait at Diogi's/Jogi' bund.

Deknni 14

FARO DILE VO RE BABA

1. Faro dile vo re baba
    Faro dile vo
    Te papinnin koxe tumkam
    Faro dile vo

2. Zaum-um *kosim mim* re baba
    Zaum-um kosim mim
    Te priman sodun *kosim miam*
    Zaum kosim mim

1. Blows were given to you, fellow, you were hit with blows. How did that wicked woman give you blows, hit you with blows?

2. *Meaning unclear.*

Deknni 15

FONDDECHA DESIAGERY

1. Fonddecha desiagery
   Ek kolvont natsota
   Are vo
   Ox'm-oxem natsota
   Are vo
   Ox'm-oxem natsota

2. Corneticha sadary kolvont
   Ox'm-oxem morhota
   Are vo
   Pol'ngari nideta
   Are vo
   Ox'm-oxem lollota

1. A temple girl is dancing at the house of the Desai of Fonddem/Ponda. Hey! This is how she (wiggles her hips as she) dances.

2. At the sound of the bugle – this is how the naughty girl wiggles. Hey! She lies on the bed. Hey! This is how she (twists as she) rolls.

Deknni **16**

FULO MALLUNUM

1. Fulo mallunum
   Kely'm anvem satem
   Tantum ſalto
   Eko tsampem

2. Soronam rati
   Ravonom zagem
   Nomoskar kortam deva
   Tolloxi bountem

3. O y amtso devu
   Polnnum geleari
   Aum-um taka
   Govai diinom

4. Oklê-ory'tachem
   Kory alegrinom
   Oklê-ory'tachem
   Kory alegrinom

1. Wearing flowers in my hair, I made a pretty bouquet. A champak posy is all it needs now.
2. The night does not end; I will stay awake. My god, I go round the sacred basil in worship.

3. If this our god runs away, I will bear witness for him.
4. Wish the bride and groom well. Good wishes to bride and groom.

*Verse 1, champak (*Pulmeria acutifolia *or* Pulmeria acuminata; *formerly* Michelia champaca*): a beautiful tree, celebrated in Indian poetry, and cultivated around Hindu and Jain temples. It has long, oval, pointed and waved leaves, shining above, with yellow and strongly fragrant flowers, favored by women as a hair adornment.*

*Verse 2, sacred basil (*Ocimum Sanctum *or* Ocimum Hirsutum*). A plant sacred to Vaishnava Hindus, very commonly cultivated, particularly near temples and Brahmins' residences.*

Deknni 17

GE GE GE GE GE

COR 1: Ge ge ge ge ge
Ge ga saiba

Maka naka go
Maka naka go

1. E muja fulants' pormollu
   Ge ga saiba

2. E muja nakatso notu
   Ge ga saiba

3. E muja golleantuli gollxiri
   Ge ga saiba

4. E muja y atanchim kanknnam
   Ge ga saiba

5. E muja paianchim painzonnam
   Ge ga saiba

COR 2: Maka naka go
Maka naka go

6. E muja polcatso beiju
   Ge ga saiba

COR 3: Maka zai-i go
Maka zai-i go

CHORUS 1

DANCER: Take it, do please take it, sir!

LOVER: I don't want it, no, I don't want it!

1. This my flower chaplet, Take it, please sir!

CHORUS 2

LOVER: I don't want it. No, I don't want it (I don't want them)!

DANCER:
2. This nose ring of mine, do please take it, sir!
3. This necklace of mine, do please take it, sir!
4. These my bangles, do please take them, sir!
5. These my anklets, do please take them, sir!
6. A kiss from my cheek, do please take it, sir!

LOVER: Yes, I want it, yes I do!

Arnaldo de Menezes

Deknni 18

GONNESPOTI RAYA

I

1. Gonnespoti raya
   Taka salamm y amim korya
   Potrovalleo manddun taka
   Jevonn borem diuya

2. Muinnom bori garam' dovon-n
   Diutti taka lauya
   Bozonn taji korun dada
   Baintum taka sorhya

3. Supary-panom dakoun taji
   Betto y amim korya
   Lokximonnank sangun tsampeak
   Vazop taka dorya

4. Allvantulean gelolo Gonnes
   Fuim paula to pollya
   Bette' lagun pollun gela
   Orile (Horile) baintum sodya

5. Kolvontantso mello y arhun
Pursaum karhun orya
Betto taji korun dada
Orile baintum sorhya

II

6. Inglezany'm bandily' reilvei agim-
Garhy Bomboim-Puneam oili
Ankvar cherhvanly' garhamorhi
Botller bountai barabori

7. Paicha gelea xezra o menddo
Bab to tsolo cazra'
Ituly'm ozranch'm bens randdugean
Hailem eka ozra'

8. Kailim' galnum mas go randdgea
Karhinom tuji oso
Eki torsady man-n go randdgea
Kurhke kot-tol'm sato

9. Kalle kaprhachi kas go randdgea
Jivachi sorhy tum aso
Eki torsady man-n go randdgea
Kurhke kot-tol'm sato

10. Sangeary vazlam xingo, muja
Kanantum pol-llam nazo
Inga kitem kot-t' *banchetu*
Mosto *madar-chetu*

11. Guerra oicha' oitai y amim
Diso ol-leai pondra
Guerro vencer kory ga deva
Rama Rama-Tsondra

I

1. Let us greet (lit. make our salams to) king Ganapati. Let us arrange leaf garlands, and serve him a good meal.
2. Let us keep him for a whole month at home, and light wick lamps to him. Singing devotional songs of praise, let us throw him into a well.
3. Showing him betel leaf and nut, let us pay him a visit. Let us tell Lakshman and have bands play for him at the champak tree.
4. Ganapati has fled through the arum groves; let us find out where he has gone. He has run away because of our visits. Let us look for him in Hari's well.
5. Let us get a crowd of dancing girls and take him in a procession. Let us pay him a visit and then throw him into Hari's well.

II

6. The English have built a railway. The train (lit. fire-vehicle) has been taken all the way to Bombay and Pune. Unmarried girls have gone wild and cooks escort them.
7. ... *Meaning unclear...* All this property worth many thousands the scoundrel let go for a paltry thousand!
8. You slut, I'll put your flesh in a pan and melt the fat from it. With a single stroke, you wicked broad, I'll chop you into seven pieces!
9. You whore, you in the black sari with its fold between your legs, give up all yearning for life. I'll slice you to seven pieces, you vile thing, with one stroke of the sword!
10. The horn has sounded in Sangem; its sound has fallen into my ears. What are you doing here, you sister-raper, you impudent mother-raper!
11. We are going to the wars. We have only fifteen days left. Oh god, please win the war for us, oh Rama, Ramachandra!

ARNALDO DE MENEZES(1863-1917), composer of the deknni, is one of the three great composers of the Mando, the other two being Gizelino Rebelo (1875-1931) and Torquato de Figueiredo (1876-1948). The Mando appears to have originated in the 1840s, two decades before Arnaldo was born, but it was he who gave it its standard form and its widest expression.

Arnaldo is the author of several other compositions, like religious works, miscellaneous songs, dulpods, even an anthem-like piece, and this deknni. Its second part is not his: the swear words it contains, "banchetu" and "madarchetu", derived from Hindi, suggest that its author was a Bombay emigrant. It seems reasonable to suppose that Arnaldo composed his part of the deknni around 1880, and that the second part was put together around 1895.

Verse 4, "arum groves"(allum, Colocasia Antiquorum), *perennial herbs with most of the leaves arranged about the root. The flowers cluster one above another on the lower part of a common stalk, without having a separate stalk for each flower. They are enclosed in leaf-like appendages resembling petals. Arum leaves are large and nearly oval; the lower part of each leaf is arrow-shaped. The appendages of the flowers are pale yellow on a green base.*

Verse 6, "railway," built by British engineers from 1882 to 1888.

Verse 11, "wars." Probably the revolt of the Maratha soldiers of 1895. which lasted from September to November.

Deknni 19

JAMNAM POROBAJA

Jamnam porobaja
Ruibam surya
Donanfire Goklla baze
Amanam baze
Donam fire
Ruibam surya
Ruibam surya

On the opposite side of the Yamuna, the... sun... on the side of Gokula. On our side... the... sun, the... sun.

The language of this piece is not Konkani. Our translation is conjectural.

Deknni 20

KAINCH KARANN NAM

Kainch karann nam
Morhkeam' tandull nam
Potta' łagoly' buko
Y atam y amim vosum' ya re
Baiku' mellunko
Baiku rupoi ditai ratiko
Baiku y amgery tum y ek vellu ravo

For no reason at all, there is no rice in the pot. I am hungry. Let us now go and call on the harlots. The bawd charges a rupee a night. Do stay one night with us, call girl.

Deknni 21

KAZOLL KUKUMM MANNYKA' PANNIM

1. Kazoll kukumm mannyka' pannim
 Bancu rigla motianim

2. E gorachi riti fotti
 Navan vosnam dhormanchi

3. Gounllea' gara geloly' korhen
 Tannom lagli dudachi

4. Etonn'm-oitonn'm moskory' kortam
 Moskory' nuim re kamanchi

Gonçal' babu tiketty zala
Don kalliz toru
Re randdgea nam tuk' ed' baru

1. Lampblack, vermilion, jewel water, the stool encrusted with gems.

2. The ways of this house are wicked. I will not go there for morality's sake.

3. I went to the cowherd's house, and there felt like a drink of milk.

4. I make fun as I come and go, and quite pointless jokes they are!

Young Gonçalo has become stubborn (?), his mind and heart large (?). Have you no care, you rascal?

Deknni 22

KOLVONTAM Y AMIM PORVOTAVELIM

I

1. Kolvontam y amim
   Porvotavelim
   Vatto visrunum y amcha
   Marvam' sampol-llim

2. Vatto visrunum
   Murgonvam paulim
   Maxttora baban y amkam
   Apounum velim

COR: Tumy'm amkam siripon-nnaim go
Benddan vankrhelim

II

3. Ton-neam konddeachim
   Patollam vellam
   Karhunko borim y amim
   Konkonnim maram

4. Amim osoitam/osoitai
   Parhelim garam
   Sonsar barhkanim mul-llol'
   Gonsally'm disolam

5. Ful-llea pantteachem
   Ot-tango ul-lam
   Durhu naxleari barhkany
   Diyai ge solam

DANCING GIRLS

1. We are the dancing girls from the holy Mountain. We lost our ways and ran into a bunch of *mhars*.

2. We lost our way and arrived in Murgoum/ Mormugão. There the boss called us and took us with him.

CLIENTS: You are of no use to us, with your crooked hips!

BASKET WEAVERS

3. To peel off thin shavings from your bamboos – that is what we Hindu *mhars* are good at.

4. We live in abandoned houses. What we call the world, lady, seems to us a worthless towel gourd.

5. You still owe us half a *tanga* or our last basket. If you have no money, give us dried fruit peels.

Verse 1. Porvot (Sanskrit parvata*), the holy Mountain in south Goa, sacred to Chandranatha, Lord of the Moon.*

Verse 4. Towel gourd (gonsallem, Luffa Acutangula *or* Luffa Amar*). One of a kind of fibrous fruits once used as flesh rubbers (hence the name). Its leaves have each five to seven lobes, and are softly hairy when young. Its flowers are middle-sized and bright yellow. The fruit has ten sharp ridges, growing on a plant which is a pretty climber, sometimes found in hedges. Its flowers open in the afternoon.*

Verse 5, dried fruit peels (solam). Skins of fruits like the wild mangosteen (birondd, Garcinia Indica*) and peelings of the mango, dried in the sun, and sometimes cured in salt. These peels serve as condiments in curries and sauces.*

Deknni 23

KUXTTOBA

1. Kuxttoba
    Miraxi Indietso
    Terroru Gointso
    Conflit povatso
    Inimig bottatso!

2. "Aik ge y aka
Atam kitem sangum tuka
Bettol'm mujem odruxtt
Bettol'm mujem kopal
Boguncha' Arsenal!"

3. "Are muja Ori/Hori
Muja paianch' geleai kati
Zain aum zain
Zatinum bhanddari
Kapinaxleary gountti!"

4. "Goiam oche vattery
Vankrheo-tinkrheo mero
Juizacha sent'san
Bottache rojen
Paiam' galeai sankllo!"

"Ai, damike sunttun
Bottachi gountti re kapin!"

Bottako mal-lo munn y aple garant
Tsoukox' pavoili sogle ganvant
Ofisy (oficio) pattoili fisicalank
Kuxttoba' galunk y Arsenalant

POET 1. Kuxttoba, India's heir, Goa's terror, cause of conflict among people, the Brahmin priest's mortal enemy!

KUXTTOBA 2. Hear me, elder sister! What can I tell you? I have met my misfortune; I have met my fate (lit. forehead) – to suffer the humiliation of the Arsenal!

3. Oh, my dear Hari, the skin of my feet has peeled off. May my caste not be *bhandari* if I do not hack off that head!

4. On the road to Goa, the ridges of the fields are zigzagged. By the judge's verdict, by the Brahmin priest's permission, they have clamped my feet in chains.

Oh! By breaking out of the prison, I shall cut off the Brahmin priest's head!

POET: Because he had killed the Brahmin priest in his own house, they carried out the search in every village. They issued an order to the officials – to throw Kuxttoba into the Arsenal prison.

The story of the "poetic and heroic Kuxttoba," as the contemporary poet Frederico Diniz d'Ayalla [1860-1923] describes him, is narrated by the latter as follows:

"A bott (Brahmin priest) had stained his [Kuxttoba's} family's honor [by raping (his brother's?) widow; this happened in 1868]. Kuxttoba vowed that he would avenge himself, and looked for an opportunity to punish the shameless Brahmin. The bott, to see himself free from the hand that threatened him, suborned witnesses to impute a crime of some sort to his enemy slanderously [that they had seen Kuxttoba and his father murder someone in the woods]. Persons [three in number, as required by law] were not wanting who, moved by indignation against the sacrilegious man who threatened to lay hands on the person of the priest, agreed to cooperate with the impudent Brahmin's contemptible plot. Kuxttoba [and his father], with manacled feet, groaned for long in prison, being condemned to hard labor for an imaginary crime. One day he broke his fetters and disappeared. After a few days, the news reached the capital [Panaji] that Kuxttoba had put himself at the head of a powerful gang, and that he was laying everything waste and in ruins. He made himself a terror of the New Conquests [and of the Old too], and his dread name was sung by the people as that of a legendary villain. In fact, he was a skillful guerilla and a brave hillman. He broke out of prison as a tiger out of a cage, frothing with fury and breathing revenge. He [had] spent his days in prison planning a just crime; when least expecting it, the bott was at Kuxttoba's feet, his heart stabbed and his body in pieces. Afterwards, Kuxttoba assembled a body of soldiers and concealed himself in jungles, from where he would now and then lead his band to pillage, assassinate and destroy. The fatality of things had turned him from a hero to a highwayman. However, with his thirst for vengeance quenched, the wave of blood which had inebriated his brain receded before the pale vision of remorse. He wished to reform, to return to the loved home for which he had turned murderer and brigand, but could not, because he fell into the hands of the law's minions [as he was leaving the house of a whore (in police pay?)

on the night of June 13, 1871], who killed him in a cowardly fashion."Goa antiga e moderna, Lisbon 1888, ch. 1, p. 16.

Our deknni does not seem to be aware of Kuxttoba's death, nor apparently of his uprising in 1869; we can therefore assume it to have been composed before that date.

Line 5, Arsenal. An irregular monastery-like building (destroyed) on the banks of the river Mandovi in the city of Velha Goa, where ships were repaired and armed, and ammunition produced, up to the third quarter of the 18th century. Its maintenance then became a burden, and its buildings in serious disrepair. It was abolished in 1869, the very year of Kuxttoba's uprising.

Deknni 24

MUJI MAIM-IM BOISOLEA

1. Muji maim-im boisolea
   Adolleri vo
   Muji maim-im boisolea
   Adolleri mum

2. Tivi xindita y eki
Munddolli mum
Tivi xindita y eki
Munddolli

1. My mother is sitting on the slicing stool, on the slicing stool.

2. She is slicing an onion, an onion.

Deknni 25

MUZO FULANTSO PORHU

1. Muzo fulantso porhu
Sanddol' deva
Muzo fulantso porhu
Sanddol' deva!
Age nari tuzo fulantso porhu
Matea sori!

2. Muzo nakatso notu
Sanddol' deva
Muzo nakatso notu
Sanddol' deva!
Age nari tuja nakatso notu
Naka sori!

3. Muja golleantu' gollxiri
Sanddily' deva
Muja golleantuli gollxiri
Sanddily' deva!
Age nari tuja golleantuli gollxiri
Gomttea sori!

4. Muja atachim kanknnam
Sanddoly'm deva
Muja atachim kanknnam
Sanddoly'm deva!
Age nari tuja y atanchim kanknnam
Ata' sori!

5. Mujim paianchim painzonnam
Sanddoly'm deva
Mujim paianchim painzonnam
Sanddoly'm deva!
Age nari tuja paianchim painzonnam
Paiam' sori!

DANCER: 1. My chaplet of flowers, oh god, has been lost. I've lost my chaplet of flowers, oh god!

LOVER: Oh woman, your chaplet of flowers is there on your head!

DANCER: 2. My ring from my nose, oh god, has been lost. I've lost my nose ring, oh god!

LOVER: Oh woman, your nose ring is there on your nose!

DANCER: 3. My necklace from my neck, oh god, has been lost. I've lost my necklace, oh god!

LOVER: Oh woman, your necklace is there on your neck!

DANCER: 4. My bangles on my hand, oh god, have been lost.
I've lost my bangles, oh god!

LOVER: Oh woman, your bangles are there on your hand!

DANCER 5. My anklets on my feet, oh god, have been lost.
I've lost my anklets, oh god!

LOVER: Oh woman, your anklets are there on your feet!

Deknni 25, Variant 1

MUJEM PAIANCHEM PAINZONN. Variant 1 of MUZO FULANTSO PORHU

I

1. *Mujem paianchem painzonn*
   Sanddlem deva
   Mujem paianchem painzonn
   Sanddlem deva

2. *Mujim nakachim notim*
   Sanddlim deva
   Mujim nakachim notim
   Sanddlim deva

3. *Muzo tambrhelo xelo*
   Gelo deva
   Muzo tambrelo xelo
   Gelo deva

II

4. *Ge ge ge ge ge*
Ge ga saiba

Maka naka go
Maka naka go

5. *E muja fulantso pormoll*
Ge ga saiba
Maka naka go
Maka naka go

Deknni 25, Variant 2

MUZO MOGATSO POTI.
Variant 2 of MUZO FULANTSO PORHU

1. *Muzo mogatso poti*
Melo deva
Muzo mogatso poti
Melo deva

2. *Muzo koplatso kukumm*
Velo/Gelo deva
Muzo koplatso kukumm
Velo/gelo deva

3. *Mujim kouxeachim/mateachim fulam*
Velim/Gelim deva
Mujim kouxeachim/mateachim fulam
Velim/Gelim deva

4. *Muji golleachi gollxiri*
   Veli/Geli deva
   Muji golleachi gollxiri
   Veli/Geli deva

5. *Mujem nakachem notim*
   Velem/Gelem deva
   Mujem nakachem notim
   Velem/Gelem deva

Deknni 26

NAUM MUJEM ERIKETI (HENRIQUETA)

Naum mujem Eriketi
   Angako gatylea jaqueti
   Alfiada' dilynam feti
   Burgim tugê' zatrich
   Burgim tugê' zatrich
   Diuchi mul-llea banqueti

My name is Henriqueta. I've put on a jacket and have not paid the tailor's bill. When children are born to you, when you have children, we have planned to host a banquet.

Deknni 27

OIRY OIRY OIRY DOGRA'

1. Oiry oiry oiry dogra'
   Udoko kongrem
   Kolvont naum Mogrem dada
   Kolvont naum Mogrem

2. Oiry oiry oiry dogra'
   Udoko ubem
   Kolvont naum Subem dada
   Kolvont naum Subem

3. Oiry oiry oiry dogra'
   As' y eky okolo
   Tiko' y ek segred y as' re
   Bomblê' sokolo

4. Oiry oiry dograri
   Yetai mukari
   Randdanle cumpary' dada
   Randdanly' cumpari

1. High, high up on the hill the water ripples (lit. is curled). The dancing girl's name is Mogrem (Jasmine), sir, her name is Mogrem.

2. High, high up on the hill the water shoots up (is vertical). The dancing girl's name is Subem, sir, her name is Subem.

3. High, high up on the hill, there is a bride, and she has a secret below her navel.

4. High, high up on the hill, the widows' lovers are coming forward, sir, the widows' friends.

Deknni 28

PAIAM' PAINZONNAM

1. Paiam' painzonnam
   Nakako notem
   Sor' sor' sor' kon-nak' bai
   Paianchem karhi zotem

2. Ailol' Kuxttoba

1. Anklets on the feet, a ring through the nose. Don't make that scraping noise (sor, sor, sor) on the ground, dear girl. Take your sandals off.

2. Kuxttoba came...

Deknni 29

PONNJECHA PATTEARY MAIM

1. Ponnjecha patteary maim
   Corneti vazota, oi, oi, oi
   Ponnjecha patteary maim cornete vazota

2. Cornetich' sadary maim
   Xiuntem natsota, oi, oi, oi
   Cornetich' sadary maim Xiuntem natsota

1. At the Panaji square, mother, the bugle is sounding, yes, yes, yes! At the Panaji square, mother, the bugle is sounding.

2. At the sound of the bugle, mother, [the dancing girl] Xiuntem [Chrysanthemum] is dancing, yes, yes, yes! At the sound of the bugle, mother, Xiuntem is dancing.

Deknni 30

PORTUGALA' SAUN

Portugala' saun
Aila ek firngi
Bollsantum galnum dada
Ottra rupoi-i

A white man has come from Portugal, sir, with eighteen rupees in his pocket.

Deknni 31

SAIBA RAYAN BANDU GATILA

1. Saiba rayan bandu gatila
   Sogottu loku punji
2. Tea gurngutticha mostokim
   Tsamim-mamim, amim dogaim ubim
3. Bangrho nouro, perhi nouri
   Konkaro tanchi derhi
4. Kansou-u panniyam' gito gai-i
   Kolo kot-ta nachi
5. Barik nachi
   Nachi nachi nachi nachi nachi

1. The lord king has issued a proclamation. All the people are crowded together.
2. In front of the beetle (lit. at the beetle's head) stand both of us, tsamim-mamim.
3. The mackerel is the groom, and the shad the bride. The partridge is the best man.
4. The tortoise, in the water, is singing a song. The fox is doing a dance.
5. Dance deftly, dance and dance and dance and dance and dance!

Deknni 31, Variant 1

AILE DONGURI
Variant 1 of SAIBA RAYAN BANDU GATILA

1. *Aile donguri*
   Pele donguri
   Kolo korta nachi
   Dongureche donguri
   Fulolam moguri
   Sogottu loku punji

2. *Mazoru bosulam*
   Tsauchaku taku
   Undiru tsauta lonnim
   Lonnientum burholi
   Sonddi ga undira
   Tsanim marita mitti

Deknni 31, Variant 2

SAIBA RAYANUM BANDU GATILA. Variant 2 of SAIBA RAYAN BANDU GATILA

1. *Saiba rayanum bandu gatila*
   Sogottu loku punji

2. *Gurungutto ketti barik vaji*
   Saozo maritati

3. *Bangrho nouro, perhi nouri*
   Konkaro tanchi derhi

4. *Vagullem eklem mattou-u gorhi*
   Sangallo tachi merhi

5. *Kansou-u panniyam' gito gai-i*
   Kolo kot-ta nachi

Deknni 32

SAIBA TANDDELA

Saiba tanddela
Amkam tum pau ga
Lognantso sangorh
Amkam tum darhy ga
Rupiachem agttem
Amkam tem zai ga
Em amchem magnnem
Augorho nuim ga

Ferryman, sir, please carry us over. Please send us the wedding raft, too. We need that silver brazier. This request of ours is not a hard one, sir.

Line 3, "wedding raft" (sangorh), a raft made of two small single-masted boats joined together by logs, with some space left between.

Deknni 33

SATTI OZRANCH' BENS MUJE ADINOM

1. Satti ozranch'm bens muje adinom
   Sonn'm sonn'm sonn'm sonn'm sa!
   Tazo tivantto tuka go diinom
   Sonn'm sonn'm sonn'm sonn'm sa!
      Ago Boiru tuje vinnem
      Suk maka nam

2. Battantu' bab maka Mannykeantum ota
   Sonn'm sonn'm sonn'm sonn'm sa!
   Tum huim-m san Tallantum pauta
   Sonn'm sonn'm sonn'm sonn'm sa!
   Nak' zaloly' visy (vicios) baba tuka konnom re xikoita?
      Ago Boiru tuje vinnem
      Suk maka nam

3. Maim-m muntta maka sun ge muje
   Sonn'm sonn'm sonn'm sonn'm sa!
   Tondda' palou dory ge lojê
   Sonn'm sonn'm sonn'm sonn'm sa!
      Aba re, aba re
      Tsoi tsoi tsoi tsoiyeai muje dolle
      Tuja mogan rorhunum suzoile
      Ago Boiru tuje vinnem
      Suk maka nam

4. Maim-im muntta maka lognam' soru
 Sonn'm sonn'm sonn'm sonn'm sa!
 Bangrach' vinnem gor za toru
 Foto-quimaum nexileari
 Sonn'm sonn'm sonn'm sonn'm sa!
 Kouxeachi pakolli
  Aba re, aba re
  Tsoi tsoi tsoi tsoiyeai muje dolle
  Tuja mogan rorhunum suzoile
  Ago Boiru tuje vinnem
  Suk maka nam

1. I own property worth sixty thousand. (Hear my wealth jingle – *sonn'm sonn'm sonn'm sonn'm sa!*). I will give you a third of that. Besides, I will support you.

 Hey there, hey there! Look, see how I have reddened my eyes through weeping for love of you!

2. Our young master from the Batt goes to Mannkem [on the opposite bank of the river]. (*Sonn'm sonn'm sonn'm sonn'm sa!*) From there he gets to the Tall [where the whores are]. Who taught you these needless vices, boy?

 Hey there, hey there! Look, see how I have reddened my eyes through weeping for love of you! Boiru, my dear, without you there is no joy for me!

3. My mother says to me, "Oh, my daughter-in-law, (*Sonn'm sonn'm sonn'm sonn'm sa!*) hold your sari's end to you face (cover your face with your sari) for shame!" If you kneel in the middle of the hall, I shall fall at your feet.

 Hey there, hey there! Look, see how I have reddened my eyes through weeping for love of you! Boiru, my dear, without you there is no joy for me!

4. My mother says to me, the marriage string (of pearls?), (*Sonn'm sonn'm sonn'm sonn'm sa!*), without gold the house is doing great. When she puts on the fota-quimão she looks like a petal of the screwpine flower.

 Hey there, hey there! Look, see how I have reddened my eyes through weeping for love of you! Boiru, my dear, without you there is no joy for me!

Verse 2, "Batt,"an area in the ward of Kon'jem in Kurhtori, near the bank of the Zuari, mentioned in at least one dulpod.

Verse 2, "Tall," the area of Xirvorhem where the temples are situated, and which contained the residences of the temples' dancing girls, who offer sexual services to desirous clients.

Verse 4, "fota-quimão."Better known as torhop-baz or bazu-torhop. It was the traditional costume of Christian Brahmin women, a combination of the long-armed blouse and the sarong – with a broad vertical band added to center of the latter garment and a horizontal one round its lower end. The word torhop itself is derived from the Kannada tarhapu, meaning an apron. The more costly varieties of the torhop-baz are embroidered with gold thread and are known as the fota-quimão.

Verse 4, "screw pine flower"(kovaso, Pandanus Odoratissimus*).*

Deknni 34

SOKANNY'M FURHEM UTTUN CHERH'M MUJ'M

1. Sokanny'm furhem uttun cherh'm muj'm
   San-nim mat-talem
   Sannam sannam sannam (sannam) sa !
   Tem maka deknam furhem
   San-nintum nipolem

2. Sokanny'm furhem uttun cherh'm muj'm
   Vatlleo ganxtalem
   Sannam sannam sannam (sannam) sa !
   Tem maka deknam furhem
   Vatllintum nipolem

3. Sokanny'm furhem uttun cherh'm muj'm
   Tambio ganxtalem
   Sannam sannam sannam (sannam) sa !
   Tem maka deknam furhem
   Tambiantum nipolem

Cherh'm cherh'm cherh'm kumparilem
Cherh'm cumparilem
Chintloly'm kamm zaly'm ga mugelem !

1. Rising up early in the morning, the girl was sweeping the floor (and this is how it sounded: *sannam sannam sannam sannam sa!*). No sooner did she see me, than she hid inside the broom!

2. Rising up early in the morning, the girl was scrubbing the dishes (*Sannam sannam sannam sannam sa!*). No sooner did she see me, than she hid behind those dishes!

3. Rising up early in the morning, the girl was scrubbing the little copper pot (*Sannam sannam sannam sannam sa!*). No sooner did she see me, than she hid inside the pot!

> The girl, my mate's girl, my comrade's girl. I got from her what I wanted (lit. the work I had thought of took place)!

Deknni 35

TENDDULECHIM TENDDULIM

COR: Tenddulechim tenddulim
Bara ga deva deva
Tenddulechim tenddulim bara

1. Muzo poti naim-im gara
Ga deva deva
Poti naim-im gara

2. Muja hankeantum gatulim
Ora ga deva deva
Hankeantum gatulim ora

CHORUS: The tenddulis of the tendduli creeper are twelve, oh god, oh god! The tenddulis of the tendduli creeper are twelve.

1. My lord is not at home, oh god, oh god! My lord is not at home.

2. They were thrown into my lap, oh god, oh god! They were thrown into my lap.

Chorus: *Tenddulim*
See *Deknni* 2

Deknni 36

VAINGEM CAZAR ZATA MUNN

I

1. Vaingem cazar zata munn
    Vaingem cazar zata munn

2. Misangen tambrhem kelam tondd
    Misangen tambrhem kelam tondd

3. Poddollean orxem kelam sondd
    Poddollean orxem kelam sondd

4. Bobran getilam boleponn
    Bobran getilam boleponn

II

5. Vernencha tolleant
    Fulol'm y ek sallok
    Dulgealy' cazra
    Keullean geun yet'm mul-ll'm ballok

6. At'm tum, at'm tum
    At'm tum, at'm tum
    At'm tum nats go Dulgea
    Keulleach' barabori

1. Because the eggplant is getting married, because the eggplant is getting married;

2. The chili has reddened her face, the chili has reddened her face;

3. The snake gourd has turned up her nose, the snake gourd has turned up her nose:

4. And the pumpkin has resigned herself [slumped down in resignation], the pumpkin has resigned herself.

5. In the lake at Vernnem/Verna a lotus has bloomed. The temple servant has promised to come to Dulgem's wedding – with a baby.

6. Now, now, now, Dulgem, dance with the temple guy!

Deknni 36

Variant of VAINGEM CAZAR ZATA MUNN

I

1. *Vaingem cazar zata munn*
   Vaingem cazar zata munn

2. *Misangen tambrhem kelam tondd*
   Misangen tambrhem kelam tondd

3. *Poddollean orxem kelam sondd*
   Poddollean orxem kelam sondd

4. *Bobran gexilam moneponn*
   Bobran gexilam moneponn

II

5. *Perhnecha dogra'*
   Fulol'm y ek sallok
   Dulgealy' cazrak
   Keullean geun yet'm mul-ll'm ballok

Deknni 37

VOKOL Y AMCHI LOKMI SORI

Vokol y amchi Lokmi sori
Sonn'm sonn'm sonn'm sonn'm sa !
Bangarachi goroz torhi
Sonn'm sonn'm sonn'm sonn'm sa !
Modlea salant dimbi gatlea
Paiem porhum' tuka

Aba re, aba re !
Tsoi tsoi tsoi tsoiyeai muje dolle
Tuja mogan rorhunum suzole

Our bride is like Lokmi/Lakshmi [goddess of wealth]. (Hear her money clink, *sonnom, sonnom, sonnom sonnom sa!)* She has little need for gold. I have knelt in the middle hall to fall at your feet. Look, look and see how red my eyes have become through weeping for love of you!

Deknni 38

XIRVORHECHIM CHERHVAM

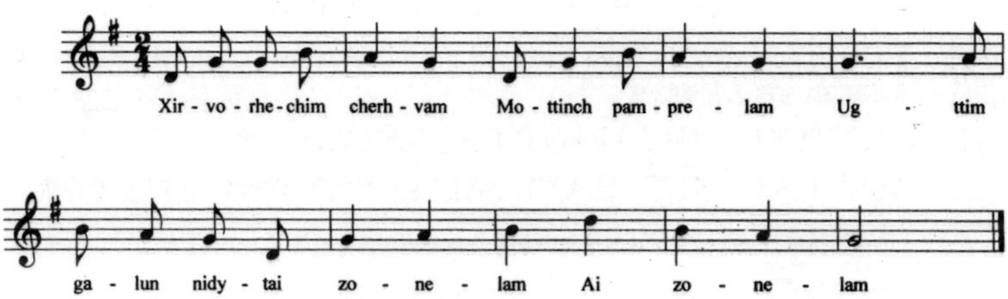

Xirvorhechim cherhvam
    Mottinch pamprelam
    Ugtim galun nidytai zonelam
    Ai ! zonelam

The girls of Xirvorhem/Siroda are great flirts; they sleep with their windows open, yes, their windows.

ALPHABETICAL LIST OF MANDO-DULPODS & DEKNNIS

Mando-Dulpods

1. ADVOGADANY'M VARHOILEAIM HARHAM
2. AITRACH' SOKANNIM MISSAKO
3 BANNALEANTUM MUZO GAUM-UM
4. CECILIO MUJEM NAUM
5. DANDDEA CAETAN BUTIQUEIRU
6. ESTUD SANDDUN BOUNTAM MUNN
7. GARANTULIM BAIRI SOT-TONNOM
8. IM TIM LOTLLE' BAMBONNAM
9. LANOM Y AUM BURGEM ASTONNOM
10. MAIM-PAI MAKA KORYTAI RE FUGARO, *Carmo Abreu & Arnaldo de Menezes*
11. RAINTUM TSOLI DINAIM KONNOM
12. SANGEARY AUM [SANKVALLE] PARHUM' GELOLIM
13. TAMBRHEM NESUN FOTO, *Arnaldo de Menezes*

Deknnis

1. AG' Y AGA SONAR XETTI

   AILE DONGURI. Variant 1 of SAIBA RAYAN BANDU GATILA
2. AJ SOMARATSO DISU
3. ALTORHI GONGA
4. ALTORHY SAN PELTORHI GELEARI

   AMCHA SOMARACHA DISA. Variant of AJ SOMARATSO DISU
5. AMIM KOLVONTAM

   ARE ARE XETTI DADA. Variant 1 of AG' Y AGA SONAR XETTI
6. ARE DEULLEA (no score)

7. AT-LAUNNEM ZALEM DADA
8. AUM SAIBA PELTORHI VOITAM
   BAVACH' BOINNIM. Variant 2 of AG' Y AGA SONAR XETTI
9. BOL-LOLY' XIDIE' MUKO NAM GA
10. BORIECHE TARI
11. BOTTU MELO
12. ERIKETY ADELAI-I (HENRIQUETA ADELAIDE)
13. ERIKETY BAI ADELAI-I (HENRIQUETA BAI ADELAIDE)
14. FARO DILE VO RE BABA
15. FONDDECHA DESIAGERY
16. FULO MALLUNUM
17. GE GE GE GE GE
18. GONNESPOTI RAYA, *Arnaldo de Menezes*
19. JAMNAM POROBAJA
20. KAINCH KARANN NAM
21. KAZOLL KUKUMM MANNYKA' PANNIM
22. KOLVONTAM Y AMIM PORVOTAVELIM
23. KUXTTOBA
   MUJEM PAIANCHEM PAINZONN. Variant 1 of MUZO FULANTSO PORHU
24. MUJI MAIM-IM BOISOLEA
25. MUZO FULANTSO PORHU
   MUZO MOGATSO POTI. Variant of MUZO FULANTSO PORHU
26. NAUM MUJEM ERIKETI (HENRIQUETA)
27. OIRY OIRY OIRY DOGRA'
28. PAIAM' PAINZONNAM
29. PONNJECHA PATTEARY MAIM
30. PORTUGALA' SAUN
31. SAIBA RAYAN BANDU GATILA
   SAIBA RAYANUM BANDU GATILA. Variant 2 of SAIBA RAYAN BANDU GATILA
32. SAIBA TANDDELA (no score)
33. SATTI OZRANCH' BENS MUJE ADINOM
34. SOKANNY'M FURHEM UTTUN CHERH'M MU'JM
35. TENDDULECHIM TENDDULIM
36. VAINGEM CAZAR ZATA MUNN
   VAINGEM CAZAR ZATA MUNN, Variant
37. VOKOL Y AMCHI LOKMI SORI
38. XIRVORHECHIM CHERHVAM